The Ultimate Guide To Become A Fashion Designer

How To Be A Successful Fashion Designer

Thomas Lewis

Table of Contents

Introduction

I want to thank you and congratulate you for purchasing the book, *"The Ultimate Guide to Become a Fashion Designer: How to be a Successful Fashion Designer"*.

This book contains proven steps and strategies on how to fulfill your dreams of becoming a fashion designer.

If you spent most of your early adult life collecting luxurious items from different fashion shops, if you read fashion books and magazines instead of your academic books, or you ran a small boutique in your family garage during your high school years, you may be one of those people who are serious about fashion.

Although fashion seems fun and interesting, it is also a cut throat business. As what Heidi Klum always say on Project Runway, your fashion career may be thriving one day but it can easily dwindle. It is also difficult to be a beginner in the fashion world as many fashion royalties and big fashion houses like Louis Vuitton, Versace, Gucci, Chanel, and Salvatore Feragamo currently rule the fashion industry.

But, nothing can compare to the feeling of having your clothes worn by thousands and even millions of people.

This book contains easy to follow guides and steps that will help you become the next big name in the fashion industry. This book outlines the specific steps and strategies that you need to adopt to become a successful fashion designer and obtain fame and fortune.

This book will help you fulfill your dream of becoming part of the glamorous and glittering world of fashion.

Thanks again for purchasing this book, I hope you enjoy it!

This document is geared towards providing exact and reliable information in regards to the topic and issue covered. The publication is sold with the idea that the publisher is not required to render accounting, officially permitted, or otherwise, qualified services. If advice is necessary, legal or professional, a practiced individual in the profession should be ordered.

- From a Declaration of Principles which was accepted and approved equally by a Committee of the American Bar Association and a Committee of Publishers and Associations.

The information provided herein is stated to be truthful and consistent, in that any liability, in terms of inattention or otherwise, by any usage or abuse of any policies, processes, or directions contained within is the solitary and utter responsibility of the recipient reader. Under no circumstances will any legal responsibility or blame be held against the publisher for any reparation, damages, or

Chapter 1: Is Fashion Design the Right Career for You?

Clothing is more than just a necessity, it a way to express oneself. People are drawn to trendy designs and patterns, and are more than willing to part with a considerable amount of money to become stylish. While fashion is for everyone, fashion design is only for a few people who have the skill, the passion, and the determination.

Before you start considering a career in fashion design, you have to determine if this is the right career for you. To become a successful fashion designer, you have to have something beyond your unwavering love for fashion. You have to be passionate about fashion and you have to have the necessary skills and temperament to make it in the fashion industry.

Here are the basic skills that you will need to become a successful fashion designer:

1. Creativity and Artistry

A fashion designer should have a strong artistic talent and must have a profound creative mind. It takes creativity and artistic talent to put together mundane and simple raw materials to become a beautiful and stylish piece of clothing. If the clothing that you would produce and design does not have a unique aesthetic design, it will not sell.

A fashion designer must have a wide imagination and must think out of the box. While fashion enthusiasts always go back to classic clothing pieces, fashion designers should never run out of original and new ideas. A fashion designer must have the ability to create something edgy and unique.

2. Solid Visualization Skills

A fashion designer is a creator much like a computer engineer, a civil engineer, a machine inventor, or an architect. A fashion designer must see the end result of their work before they even begin. As mentioned earlier, a fashion designer must have a vivid imagination. Strong visualization skill is necessary if you want to create something that is creative and new. Walt Disney once said that "If you can imagine it, it is possible".

3. Good Eye for Detail

They say love is in the details. In fashion, details are important. A unique and funky detail separates one fashion piece from the rest of the clothing in the market today. In fact, many fashion buyers and fashion enthusiasts buy a fashion piece because of a certain detail. Take the Christian Louboutin pumps as an example. These pumps became popular amongst rich women and celebrities because of the red sole.

If you want to be a great and successful fashion designer, you have to pay attention to details. You have to make each detail, unique and special. Successful designers devote so much time and energy in designing a single button or a collar or a sleeve.

4. Knowledge of Color Combinations, Quality of Fabric, and Textures

A good fashion designer must have a strong eye for color. A great fashion designer also has deep knowledge about fabrics, textiles, and textures. Luckily, this knowledge can be acquired in fashion schools. But, most successful fashion designers have natural knowledge and interest in colors and fabrics.

5. Great Illustration Skill

It is not enough that you can visualize your end product, you should also have the skill illustrate it. Great fashion designers have strong illustration and drawing skills. If you do not have the sketching skills, you will often confuse your mistresses and pattern makers. As a result, your output will be different from what you have imagined. Some great fashion designers illustrate their designs using a computer. Some do it manually. But, the bottom line is you have to have strong drawing and sketching skills to create great pieces and become successful in the fashion industry.

6. Good Team Player

A fashion designer works in a team. Because of this, a great fashion designer must be a good team player. She must have great interpersonal skills and can get along with different kinds of people. To succeed in the fashion industry, you have to have a high EQ. This means that you have to have the ability to communicate your preference in a respectful manner. Many fashion designers, fashion editors, and fashion models are known for rude behavior. In fact, this behavior is often depicted in television shows like Project Runway and movies like The Devil Wears Prada. But, to make it big in the fashion industry, you have to have charisma and you should get along with your colleagues. Most successful fashion designers such as Roberto Cavalli, Christian Louboutin, Manolo Blahnik, and Gianni Versace are known for their strong people skills. As a designer, you will not get anything done without the help of the seamstress, patternmakers, raw materials suppliers, and even models. You have to get along with the other members in your team.

7. Knowledge on Fashion Trends

A fashion designer must be serious about fashion. If you want to become a successful fashion designer, you have to have solid knowledge about the "ins" and "outs" of the fashion industry. You must know the current trends and style. At the end of the day, a fashion designer must know what type of design sells. If you do not have enough knowledge about the current trends, you may produce something that is "out of style". Creating something that is hideous and out of style is the easiest way to fail in the world of fashion.

8. Strong Communication Skills

Designers deal with clients and suppliers all the time. If you do not have strong communication skill, you may be misunderstood by your suppliers, clients, and even the ruthless fashion journalists and critics. A fashion designer must have a strong communication skill in order to succeed in a cut-throat world of fashion. A fashion designer has to be a good negotiator and negotiation requires strong communication skills.

9. Competitiveness

If you want to be a successful fashion designer, you have to have a strong competitive spirit. The fashion industry is highly competitive. The only way to survive in this competitive and "dog eat dog" industry is a strong desire to be one step ahead of the other designers. To become successful in the fashion industry, you have to outwit and outdo your competitors. You have to have a strong desire to win and to always be one step ahead of the others.

10. Business Skills

At the end of the day, the glamorous and glitzy world of fashion is an industry. Its goal is not only to create innovative and beautiful clothing, but to ultimately make money. Fashion designers are usually employed in big fashion houses. But, if you want to become big in the world of fashion, you have to create and sell your own line. Many fashion designers hire business managers. But, it is a huge advantage if you have excellent business skills.

A wise designer should not produce something that would look beautiful, but would cost $2000 to produce. That is just silly. Successful designers produce a $100 dress and sell it for $1000. If you are new in the fashion industry, you may need a help of an investor or a venture capitalist to produce an initial capital. You must also create samples and create marketing strategies. You should also be able to negotiate with the suppliers to get the best materials for a very reasonable price. You should also be able to track your cost versus your expenses to ensure that you are making profits.

At the end of the day, fashion is a business and to become a player in this industry, you have to have basic business knowledge and skills.

Chapter 2: The Basic Principles in Fashion Design

If you want to become a successful fashion designer, you have to learn and understand the basic and important principles in fashion design.

Here are the basic principles in fashion design that you have to know by heart:

1. Emphasis

Emphasis is important because it creates a center of interest and it ultimately grabs the interest of the potential buyers of the garment. Emphasis is called the Focal Point in fashion design. There are many techniques that fashion designers use to emphasize a feature of a fashion accessory or a garment. Designers may apply techniques such as embellishment, prints, peplums, cutouts, or ruffles to create emphasis. Some designers use color contrast and exaggerated designs to create emphasis.

Emphasis is also used by fashion designers to highlight a specific part of the client's body. If the client wants to emphasize her shoulders, the designer could design an off-shoulder or strapless dress. If the client wants to emphasize her cleavage, the designer could design a dress that has a very low neckline.

2. Symmetrical and Asymmetrical Balance

In fashion design, balance can be achieved with the use of the garment's features such as hemlines, seams, and necklines. Most fashion designers apply the symmetrical or formal application of balance. The symmetrical balance is also called as mirror balance. However, every now and then, designers apply the asymmetrical or informal balance. One classic example of this is the "Venus cut". The asymmetrical balance is more tricky, but it is also more exciting and interesting. As a designer, you have to be careful when to apply asymmetrical balance because if this is used inappropriately, the garment will really look bad. For example, a Venus cut dress may look great, but a one shouldered jacket is definitely a fashion disaster.

3. Proportion

Proportion is a very important principle in fashion design. The size of different design components of a garment must look good together.

Proportion is generally defined as the ratio of a part to the whole. Proportion involves sizes, shape, and visual weight of a design component. For a design to be proportional, things must look just right. Here are the several principles under proportion:

1. Greek proportion

2. Palladian Proportion

3. Measured Proportion

In fashion design, unequal parts are usually more pleasing to the eye than equal parts.

4. Unity

For a design to look good, the design components must be in perfect harmony. If this principle is applied effectively in the design, each design component enhances the other components.

Chapter 3: Getting Ready with Self Study

There is no one way to succeed in the fashion industry. There are different paths that you can take. Many millionaire fashion designers are self-taught. One excellent example is James Lillis, the founder of Black Milk clothing. James Lillis has no formal training in fashion design. He also has no background in retail. Coco Chanel, Salvatore Ferragamo, and Gianni Versace also have no formal training in fashion design. They just worked with many seamstresses. Manolo Blahnik also do not have formal training in fashion design, he even took Law and later took Architecture.

If you plan to go to fashion school, you have to get ready by teaching yourself the basics in fashion design. But, if you do not have enough funds or means to go to fashion school, no need to worry. You can teach yourself how the basics in fashion design.

Here are some steps that you should take to teach yourself the basics in fashion design:

1. Learn the ins and out of the fashion industry

You have to be knowledgeable about the fashion industry. You have to know the latest trends by reading a lot of fashion magazines. You have to know the colors and designs that are dominant in the market today. A good fashion designer can forecast fashion trends.

2. Find Fashion school syllabus and find textbooks associated with the syllabus

If you cannot afford to go to a fashion school, you can search for a fashion school syllabus online. This will ensure that you will get to study everything that you need to learn about the fashion industry. This will also ensure that you will learn everything that designers who went to fashion school will learn. This will also ensure that you can compete head on with other designers who went to the elite and expensive fashion schools.

You also need to buy books that can help you learn the things and techniques that are taught in fashion schools.

3. Study a fashion illustration textbook

To learn the basics of fashion design, you have to buy and study a fashion illustration textbook. This will help you learn how to express your designs into paper. Fashion sketching textbooks will also help you simulate the look and texture of fabrics that you would like for your designs.

You should devote so much time in practicing fashion illustration and sketching. This is one of the most basic and most important skills that a fashion designer must have.

To practice and study sketching, you need the following materials:

- Sketchbook

- Pencils

- Eraser

- Ruler

- Color Markers

You will also need to have a decent desk and a comfortable chair. You need to start sketching your fashion figure or Croquis. Croquis is French for "figure". This is the figure outline where you will sketch your design on.

Then draw your design on your croquis. You can change the color of the hair or the hair styles. If you have difficulty drawing a croquis, you can print a photo of a figure that has a great pose and a body form that you would like to design for. You can trace the body shape on a new sheet of paper. When you already have your croquis, you can draw the design over it.

Be creative and do not stress too much. Your sketch does not have to be perfect right away. All you need to do is practice. Your fashion illustration books will also give you different tips that will help you improve your sketching skills.

4. Study a pattern book

Most of the time, designers hire pattern makers and seamstresses. But, it is best to learn the basics of dressmaking. To make your own patterns, you will need pattern papers, pencil, marker, tape measure, tailor square, and curve ruler. Dressmaking is a craft that takes so much practice to perfect.

You can find a good pattern book that will teach you how to create patterns for dresses, shirts, skirts, and pants.

5. Study a draping book

Draping is a sewing technique that is incorporated in many fashion designs. You could learn man draping techniques from a draping book so make sure you buy one.

But, here are the basic steps in draping:

- You should have a sketch or design prepared. A sketch will be your guide in manipulating and playing with your fabric.

- You should have a fitting muslin.

- Make your foundation fashion piece and pin it to your dress form.

- Start pinning your drapes. Draping is generally done in the front and back bodice, back skirt, and front skirt.

- Stitch the fabric to the foundation piece.

- Trim off the excess fabric and continue with the clothing construction.

6. Learn how to use a sewing machine

If you want to become a successful designer, you have to learn how to use a sewing machine. Most successful designers use expensive and heavy duty machines. You should learn how to use those. Fashion designers who do not have a degree in fashion design seam and sew their own designs in the beginning. You can teach yourself how to sew or you can ask help from your local seamstress. You can also attend vocational technical classes that teach basic sewing techniques.

These vocational classes usually teach you different types of sewing machines such as:

Mechanical Sewing Machine – This machine is operated by a rotary wheel. You have to move the dial to make some adjustments to the tension, width, or length. This machine is basic and it is also inexpensive.

Electronic Sewing Machine – You can do stuff with this machine just by pressing a button. This machine is more advanced and it is easier to use.

Computerized Sewing Machine – This is a more complex and elaborate machine. You can program several stitches into the system and it is easier to use.

7. Learn different sewing techniques

You have to learn the different sewing techniques if you want to make it in the fashion industry. There are several sewing techniques, but you have to learn the six important techniques in sewing couture:

- Hand Stitches

- French Seams

- Underlining

- Making a muslin or a test garment

- Hand-picked Zipper

- Faced Hem

- Embroidery

- Cutouts

8. Be familiar with different types of clothes and dresses

To become a popular and successful fashion designer, you should know the different styles and types of clothing.

Here are some of the types of dresses and skirts that you should be acquainted with:

- Ball Gown – A ball gown is a very formal dress that is usually elaborate and floor-length. Ball gowns are usually made of fancy fabrics.

- Evening Gown – An evening gown is a long dress worn during formal evening events.

- Cocktail Dress - It is a short semi-formal dress that is usually worn to cocktail parties.

- Wrap Dress – It is a dress that wraps around a woman's body and ties on the side. It has a V-neckline and it is flattering.

- Maxi Dress – Maxi dress is a flowing dress that has an empire waistline. The maxi dress is comfortable and it is usually worn at the beach or during tropical vacations.

- Baby Doll Dress – These are cute dresses that are not very formal. This dress is for younger women and it is perfect for petite women.

- Suit Dress – The suit dress is usually worn in the office. It has a matching jacket. These dresses are also worn during luncheon, wedding, or graduation.

- Trapeze or Shift Dress – The trapeze or shift dress fit tight at the bust and shoulder area, but it is shapeless to the hem. It was popular in the 60s.

You should also be acquainted with the following different kinds of skirts:

- A-line Skirt – This skirt clings to the waist, but it is broader at the hem. The style resembles the letter "A".

- Mermaid Skirt – The design of the skirt resembles a mermaid's tail. It is fitting from waist to knees, but, it flares out from the knees to the ankle.

- Mini Skirt – Mini skirt is a very short skirt. This skirt is inappropriate for formal meetings and the workplace.

- Macro Mini Skirt – This is a much shorter version of the miniskirt.

- Tiered Skirt – This skirt has a casual look and it has a few or several tiers.

- Tutu – This skirt is usually worn by ballerinas. But, this is also becoming a fashion trend.

- Bubble Skirt – This skirt creates a bubble effect. The bottom of the hem was tucked under.

- Pencil Skirt – This skirt hugs the body. Most pencil skirts are made of stretch materials.

- Jeans Skirt – This skirt is made of denim. This has a casual vibe and can be worn in every day activity.

- High Wasted Skirt – This skirt has a waistline that is higher than the usual waistline.

- Pleated Skirt – These skirts are filled with folds of fabric sewn from the top.

- Sarong – It is a piece of fabric that is wrapped around the body.

9. You should study the different body shapes

If you want to create and design beautiful clothing for other people, you have to master the different body shapes. This is to ensure that you will create clothes that looks great on your client. Here are the different female body shapes that you should get acquainted with:

- Straight Body Type

- Pear Body Type

- Top Hourglass Body Type

- Hourglass Body Type

- Oval Body Type

- Inverted Triangle Body Type

- Diamond Body Tyle

Here are the different male body types:

- Ectomorph

- Endomorph

- Mesomorph

To become a famous fashion designer, you have to have the basic fashion design skills. You also have to enough knowledge about colors, body shapes, stitches, patterns, and different types of garments.

Chapter 4: Different Areas of Fashion Design

Before you begin your career as a fashion designer, you have to identify which area you want to focus on. Focus is the key to success. Roberto Cavalli's initial focus is women's printed clothing. Louis Vuitton's initially focused on producing heavy duty luggages. Georgio Armani is known for his elegant suits and Manolo Blahnik is known for his beautiful women's shoes.

When you are starting your career in fashion design, you have to focus on one area first and then expand your niche as you progress.

Here are the different areas and fields in fashion design that you can focus on:

- Women's Day Wear

- Women's Lingerie

- Women's Evening Wear

- Men's Day Wear

- Men's Evening Wear

- Teenage Girl's Wear

- Teenage Boy's Wear

- Kid's Wear

- Jeans Wear

- Sports Wear

- Knitwear

- Outerwear

- Swimwear

- Performance Wear

- Accessories (Bags, Shades, Belts, Shoes, etc.)

- Bridal Wear

Most areas of fashion fall under the three major types of fashion. You have to also identify which type of fashion you want to focus on. Here are the different types of fashion that you can choose from:

Haute Couture – This is a clothing that is designed and produced on a made to measure. Haute Couture is a French Word for high sewing. A couture clothing is made to order. The clothing is produced solely for a particular client. A couture clothing generally uses high quality fabric and it is sewn with impeccable attention to every detail. Haute Couture usually caters to upmarket clients.

Mass Market – Mass market fashion supplies to a wide variety of clients and customers. The mass market usually produces ready to wear clothing that is considered trendy at the moment. These clothing is produced based on the designs of the biggest names in fashion.

The mass market clothing is produced using simpler production processes and cheap raw materials. The end product is usually cheap.

Ready to Wear- This is also called pre-a-porter. Ready to wear garments are a cross between mass market clothing and haute couture. These clothes are not made for individual clients, but these garments are designed with great care. The fabrics and the cut are also well chosen. These clothes are also produced in small quantities to ensure a level of exclusivity. These clothes are more expensive than the mass market garments. Ready to wear designs are generally showcased by different fashion houses during Fashion Week. The Fashion week takes place twice every year.

Focus is one of the most important keys of success in fashion design. Once you find the right area and type to focus on, your success is unstoppable.

Chapter 5: Enrolling in A Fashion School

The world of fashion is very competitive nowadays. Most players in the fashion design industry have a degree in fashion design and styling. If you want to have an edge in the fashion industry, you have to have a degree. If you have the time or the means, investing in a fashion design degree will yield results later on. Most huge fashion houses employ people who have formal training in fashion design.

Here are some of the fashion courses that you can study:

- Fashion Design

- Pattern Making

- Fashion Illustration

- Fashion Sewing

- Fashion Draping

- Fashion Styling

- Fashion Photography

- Fashion Make-up

- Fashion Embellishment

- Fashion Buying

- Business

- Fashion Marketing

A fashion designer must at least know the basics in pattern making, illustration, sewing, draping, styling, fashion photography, make-up, business, marketing, and embellishment.

If you want to increase your chances of being employed in top fashion houses, it is best to enroll in top fashion schools in the world. Here is the list of the top fashion schools in the world:

Parsons New School of Design

This is located in New York City and it is one of the most popular and reputable fashion schools in the world. Many famous designers such as Tom Ford, Marc Jacobs, Jason Wu, and Donna Karan graduated from this school. Tuition fee costs around $39,900 per year. This school have around 4,200 students enrolled. This school has an impressive list of instructors and connections. If you want to have a lot of career options when you graduate, you should go to Parsons, the New School of Design.

The Fashion Institute of Technology or FIT

This is considered as the MIT of fashion. It is located in New York City. It offers different programs in business, design, and marketing. Calvin Klein, Carolina Herrera, and Michael Kors graduated from this school. Tuition fees range from $3000 to $8000 per semester.

Central Saint Martins

This is one of the most popular fashion schools in Europe. This is located in London and it is part of the University of the Arts London or UAL. Alexander McQueen, Stella McCartney, and Paul Smith graduated from this school. Tuition fees range from $15,000 to $25,000.

Royal College of Art

This school is located in London and it has very high tuition fee. Tuition fees for this school amounts to about $42,000 per year. This school gives opportunity for students to work at the biggest fashion houses in the world including Louis Vuitton, Prada, Burberry, and Givenchy.

Isituto Marangoni

The main campus of this fashion school is located in Milan, but the school also has campuses in Paris and Milan. This school offers different courses in design, business, brand management, and promotion. The tuition fees range from $17670 to $24500. Domenico Dolce and Franco Moschino graduated from this school.

Ecole dela Chambre Syndicale dela Couture Parisienne

This is one of the most popular fashion schools in Paris. Its tuition fee cost around $13000 per year. Andre Courreges, Valentino, and Yves Saint Laurent graduated from this school.

You need to have a high school degree and basic knowledge in fashion design before you can enroll in any of these fashion schools. The tuition fees in these fashion schools may be expensive, but these schools will help you get employed or at least get an internship in the most popular and biggest fashion houses in the world. These schools will also give you an opportunity to work side by side with the biggest names in fashion.

Chapter 6: Fashion is a Serious Business

Before you start your career in fashion design, you have to understand that fashion is serious business. You should have a strong business sense and instinct in order to succeed in the world of fashion. Here are the business basics that you should learn to become a successful fashion designer:

1. Fashion Costing

To ensure that you will earn profits from your garments, you have to learn the basics in fashion costing. Here are some of the direct costs that you can incur in fashion design:

- Manufacturing Costs

- Raw Materials Costs

- Labor Costs

Here are the indirect costs that you will incur:

- Administrative Cost

- Financing Cost

- Marketing cost

The total indirect and direct cost of producing and marketing the product should be lower that the retail and wholesale price of the end product to make a profit.

2. Keystone Markup

To earn profits, the price of the goods must be higher than the production cost. The markup is the difference between the production cost and the price. To be successful in the fashion industry, you have to know the basics about pricing and the keystone markup.

The keystone mark-up is an amazing pricing methodology that multiplies the cost by a factor of two. It is the simplest way to mark up goods to a profitable level. The keystone markup principle holds that the production cost of the goods should be 50% of its sale price. So if you produce a $10.00 skirt, you should sell it for at least $20.00.

3. Fashion Marketing

To become successful in the fashion industry, you have to learn the basic of marketing. Before you design something, you have to ask yourself "For whom is this design for?".You have to determine your market. You have to get to know your potential buyers and clients. You have to study the preference of your target market and the amount of money that they want to spend on clothes. You should also know the basics in advertising and personal selling.

In this digital age, you should also the basics of online marketing. You can now use social media to market your products.

4. Production Management

Fashion designers usually want to become successful fashion businessmen. To be successful in the industry, you must know the basics of production management. You should know the basics in sampling and production quality control. You should also be able to identify your possible production partners.

5. Shipping, Delivery, and Merchandise Distribution

To become successful in the industry, you have to learn the basic in delivery, shipping, and merchandise distribution. You should know how to deliver, ship, and distribute your merchandise.

6. Business Planning

If you want to establish your own fashion store or fashion house later on, you have to learn the basics in business planning.

Fashion is fun and playful but at the end of the day it is still about making profits. If you want to become a key player in the fashion industry, you must have strong business strategies and tactics.

Chapter 7: Learn from the Best

To become a master in the world of fashion, you have to learn from the best. Most successful fashion designers have mentors. It is best to start as an intern or apprentice of a popular and successful designer.

You must choose a mentor who has many years of experience in the fashion industry. You should choose a mentor that clicks with you and who would be willing to invest time and effort in helping you grow as a fashion designer.

A budding fashion designer must have a mentor who has extensive knowledge of the following areas:

1. Fashion Design

You must have a mentor who has mastered the art of fashion design. Find a mentor who can teach you several fashion design techniques. Your mentor can also introduce you to other major players in the fashion industry.

2. Retail and Sales

Your mentor must have extensive knowledge in sales and retail. Your mentor could walk you through different production and marketing processes.

3. Business Development

Fashion designers are usually focused on creativity and on the design that they ignore the importance of business development. You must find a mentor who can help hone your business development skills.

4. Technology

You should train under a mentor who can help you get acquainted with several softwares and sites used in fashion design. Technology is a major component of the fashion industry nowadays. You have to be acquainted with the different technologies being used in fashion design and production to become successful in the industry.

The right mentor can help you enhance your fashion design skills and can expedite your growth in the cutthroat world of fashion.

Conclusion

Thank you again for purchasing this book!

I hope this book was able to help you learn the basics in the fashion industry. I also hope that this book was able to help you become one of the most successful players in the world of fashion design.

The next step is to apply what you have learned in this book to become one of the best fashion designers in the world will ever know.

Finally, if you enjoyed this book, then I'd like to ask you for a favor, would you be kind enough to leave a review for this book on Amazon? It'd be greatly appreciated!

Thank you and good luck!

www.ingramcontent.com/pod-product-compliance
Lightning Source LLC
Chambersburg PA
CBHW071139280526
45787CB00003B/1341